Microsoft® Excel®
Start Here
The Beginners Guide

C.J. Benton

DEDICATION

To new users of Microsoft® Excel®

Other Books Available From This Author:

1. The Step-By-Step Guide To The **25 Most Common** Microsoft® Excel® Formulas & Features

2. The Step-By-Step Guide To **Pivot Tables &** Introduction To **Dashboards**

3. The Step-By-Step Guide To The **VLOOKUP** formula in Microsoft® Excel®

4. The Microsoft® Excel® Step-By-Step Training Guide **Book Bundle**

Table of Contents

CHAPTER 1..1
An Introduction To Microsoft® Excel® 1
CHAPTER 2..4
Opening Microsoft® Excel® & The Toolbar 4
   Creating a New Spreadsheet..4
   Workbook *(definition)* 5
   Cell *(definition)* 5
   Toolbar (Ribbon) 6
   Quick Access Toolbar 7
   Save...12
CHAPTER 3..13
The Home Tab 13
   Copy..14
   Cut...14
   Paste...14
   Format Painter..16
   Font...16
   Currency - *formatting*..17
   Number & Percent - *formatting* 22
   Conditional - *formatting* 22
CHAPTER 4..24
The Insert Tab 24
   Pivot Tables 24
   Charts 25
   Illustrations...27
CHAPTER 5..30
The Page Layout Tab 30
   Print..30
   Additional print settings (Margins, Header, & Footer) 35
CHAPTER 6..38
The Data Tab...38
   Filter 38
   Sort...40
   Subtotal 41

CHAPTER 7..45
  The Review Tab..45
    Spellcheck & Thesaurus...45
    Protecting worksheets & workbooks...................................45
CHAPTER 8..48
  The View Tab 48
    Freeze Panes 48
    Split (screen) 49
CHAPTER 9..50
  Basic Formulas (Part 1)..50
    Formula 50
    Syntax...50
    Function..50
    Sum (addition) 51
    Subtraction 51
    Multiplication 51
    Division 51
CHAPTER 10..54
  Basic Formulas (Part 2)..54
    Average...54
    Minimum 54
    Maximum 54
    Count 54
CHAPTER 11..56
  Date Formulas 56
    Today, Now, & Networkdays...56
CHAPTER 12..59
  Informational Formulas...59
    Cell & Sheets...59
CHAPTER 13..60
  The Formulas Tab 60
    Insert Function..60
      CountIF Example..60
    ∑ AutoSum...63
    Function Library 63
    Trace Precedents 65

CHAPTER 14..66

Next Steps - An Introduction To Excel® Intermediate Formulas &
Features...66

    DATA VALIDATION...66

    PIVOT TABLES...67

    VLOOKUP formula 75

    IF & NESTED IF formulas 76

CHAPTER 15..78

Microsoft® Excel® Shortcuts 78

Glossary..80

Appendix A 82

  Add-Ins 82

A MESSAGE FROM THE AUTHOR 83

PREFACE

For nearly twenty years, I worked as a Data & Systems Analyst for three different Fortune 500 companies, primarily in the areas of Finance, Infrastructure Services, and Logistics. During that time I used Microsoft® Excel® extensively, developing hundreds of different types of reports, analysis tools, and several forms of Dashboards.

I've utilized many Microsoft® Excel® formulas & features, the following are the basic skills and knowledge all users should have of Microsoft® Excel®.

CHAPTER 1

An Introduction To Microsoft® Excel®

Microsoft® Excel® is the spreadsheet program that allows users to organize, report, calculate, track, and perform analysis on virtually any type of data. It is part of the Microsoft® Office® suite. You can purchase Excel® by itself or as part of the Microsoft® Office® collection. Depending on the package you purchase, the Microsoft® Office® suite typically includes four – seven of the below applications:

- **Access®** *(a database application)*
- **Excel®** *(please see definition below)*
- **OneNote®** *(a program that stores text, web links, images and other information in one place)*
- **Outlook®** *(an email application)*
- **PowerPoint®** *(a presentation / slideshow program)*
- **Publisher®** *(a tool to create professional looking flyers, advertisements, brochures, invitations etc.)*
- **Word®** *(a word processing application)*

The four most widely used applications of the suite are, **Word®**, **Outlook®**, **PowerPoint®**, and **Excel®**.

```
Excel® is the spreadsheet program
that allows users to organize,
calculate, track, and perform
analysis on virtually any type of
data.
```

According to Microsoft®, there are more than 1.2 billion[1] users of Microsoft® Office®, making it the mostly widely used office software program in the world.

With Excel®, users can create everything from simple lists and perform basic arithmetic calculations to interfacing with external databases and analyzing millions of records. Sophisticated engineering calculations and statistics can be completed in milliseconds. Repetitive spreadsheet tasks can be automated and performed with a single click of a button.

Excel® has formatting, charting, and other presentation tools that allow you to easily create professionally looking budgets, reports, estimates, invoices, lists, graphs, matrixes, virtually any type of artifact containing text, currency, charts, numeric, or time values.

Excel® is also the application that interfaces the most with other software programs and the Microsoft® Office® suite. For example, if you had names and addresses listed in Excel® you could export them into Word® and create mailing labels. From Excel® you could retrieve (import) data from Access® or a multitude of other data sources and create user friendly reports, budgets, or schedules.

There are hundreds of templates and pre-made spreadsheets available for download[2]. These can be a great time saver or serve as inspiration for designing your own spreadsheets.

---

[1] *Data from Microsoft® by the numbers, retrieved 3 October 2015*
http://news.microsoft.com/bythenumbers/planet-office

[2]*Featured Templates for Excel® provided by Microsoft®, retrieved 3 October 2015*
https://templates.office.com/en-us/templates-for-Excel#

Excel® is perhaps the most versatile and flexible application ever developed. Basic knowledge and experience with Excel® along with Word® and Outlook® are essential skills for many professions and college students.

The following pages will introduce you to the basic functionality of Excel®. We'll review the most commonly used toolbar commands, how to create a new spreadsheet, including formatting, saving, and printing. In addition to this, you'll learn the fundamental formulas that serve as the building blocks for all other calculations. The book concludes with an overview of some intermediate level Excel® formulas and features.

When finished, you'll have a solid understanding of Excel® and be ready to take the next step in your education of the Microsoft® Office® suite.

Let's begin!

CHAPTER 2

Opening Microsoft® Excel® & The Toolbar

Creating a New Spreadsheet
To open Excel®:

A. Click the '**X**' icon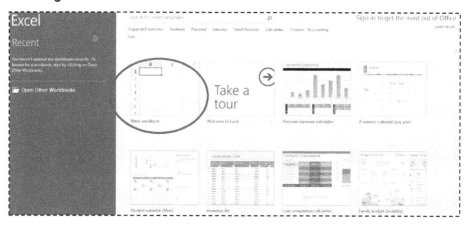

   or

B. From the **'Start'** menu, select '**All Programs**'
   1) The folder '**Microsoft® Office® *2013****'
   2) Click the program **'Excel® *2013**'**

*Depending on the version of Microsoft® Excel® you have, the <u>year</u> may be 2016, 2013, 2010, or 2007

    Once Excel® has opened, your screen will look *similar* to the following:

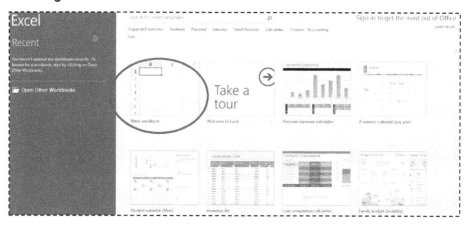

Select the **'Blank Workbook'** option.

    You'll notice pre-made templates available for download and a dialogue box to search for more previously developed files. The best practice is to learn the basic functionality of Microsoft® Excel® first before using these. Once you have a better understanding of how to use Excel®, you can modify and verify the calculations in these templates meet your requirements.

Workbook *(definition)*

Once you click the **'Blank Workbook'** option, you will have created a **'workbook'** file, made up of one or more worksheets:

> A **workbook** file is made up of one or more worksheets. Worksheets are also referred to as tabs.

Cell *(definition)*

Each worksheet contains '**cells**', displayed in a grid of *rows* and *columns*:

> A **cell** holds one piece of information such as a number, currency value, date, text, or formula.

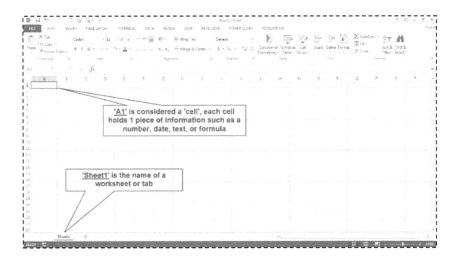

'A1' is considered a 'cell', each cell holds 1 piece of information such as a number, date, text, or formula

'Sheet1' is the name of a worksheet or tab

Toolbar (Ribbon)

The **toolbar** or what Microsoft® calls the **'ribbon'** consists of *tabs* that contain *commands*. There are eight default tabs.

Details of each tab are provided starting in chapter 3:

- File
- Home *(chapter 3)*
- Insert *(chapter 4)*
- Page Layout *(chapter 5)*
- Formulas *(chapter **13**, after the formulas chapters)*
- Data *(chapter 6)*
- Review *(chapter 7)*
- View *(chapter 8)*

Note: *the tab **'File'** does not contain commands, instead it provides information about the workbook, as well as options for **saving**, **printing**, or **exporting** the workbook file.*

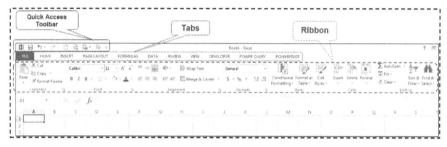

In the screenshot above, you may have noticed the ribbon contains more tabs (Developer, Power Query & PowerPivot), these are called 'Add-Ins'.

```
Add-Ins are optional tabs that
provide additional and more advanced
Excel® functionality.
```

As your Excel® experience grows beyond the basics, you may have a need for more advanced functionality. If you'd like to learn more about Add-Ins, supplementary information is proved in **Appendix A.**

Quick Access Toolbar

The **Quick Access Toolbar** sets on top of the **ribbon.** Think of this as a place to add commands that you use the most often. Commands such as *save, print, undo,* or *creating a new workbook* file. These commands stay constant, regardless of what ribbon tab is active.

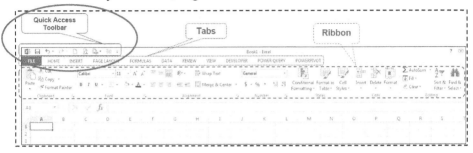

Both the **Quick Access Toolbar** and the **Ribbon** are customizable. I find it more efficient to modify the Quick Access Toolbar. However, you may prefer to change the Ribbon.

Below are the steps to remove or add buttons to both the Quick Access Toolbar and Ribbon:

1. Click the **'File'** tab
2. Select **'Options'**
3. Select either **'Quick Access Toolbar'** *or* **'Customize Ribbon'**
4. Add or Remove the buttons you wish
5. Click the **'OK'** button

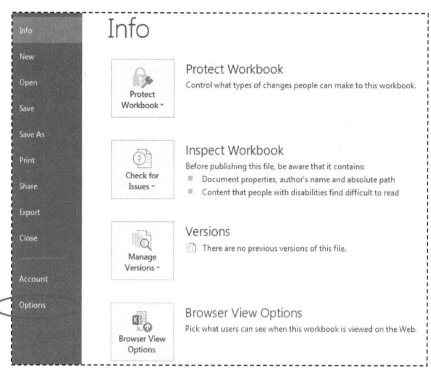

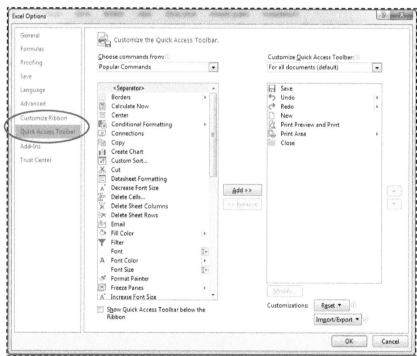

Let's take a quick look at a few more parts of the worksheet, before delving into the specifics of each tab.

The **'Name Box'** and **'Formula Bar'**:

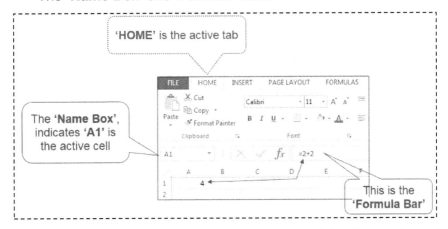

The **'Name Box'** indicates the active cell and the **'Formula Bar'** displays the **'syntax'** of a formula or a number, date, text, or currency value of the active cell.

Syntax

> **Syntax** in Excel® refers to the arrangement or order of a formula or function. All formulas & functions begin with the equal sign (=) followed by numbers or the function's name.

We'll be revisiting syntax in *chapter 9* *'Basic Formulas (Part 1) Sum, Subtraction, Multiplication, & Division'*

Lastly, across from the Quick Access Toolbar in the top left corner you'll notice a series of small icons.

The **? (question mark)**, when clicked, will launch the Microsoft® Excel® **Help** menu, you may also press (**F1**) on your keyboard to access Help screen.

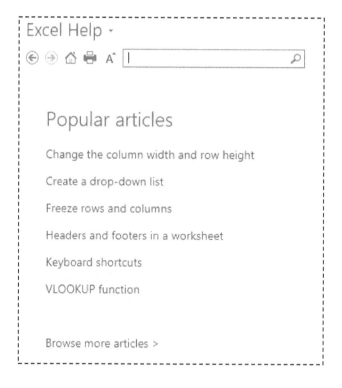

The up arrow button, when clicked, will present three ribbon options:

1. **Auto-hide Ribbon** hides the ribbon, until you click the top of worksheet to unhide
2. **Show Tabs** displays the tab name only, but not the commands
3. **Show Tabs and Commands** displays both the tab name and the commands (this is the default setting)

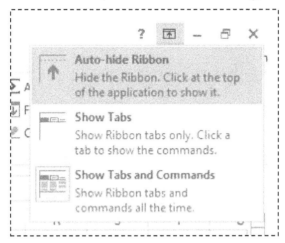

The underscore button when clicked, will **minimize** the active workbook

The double window button when clicked, will **resize** the active workbook

The cross (X) button when clicked, will **close** the active workbook (*you'll be prompted to save your file if not already done so*)

Save

To save the workbook file you just created:

1. Click the **'File'** tab
2. Click **'Save As'**

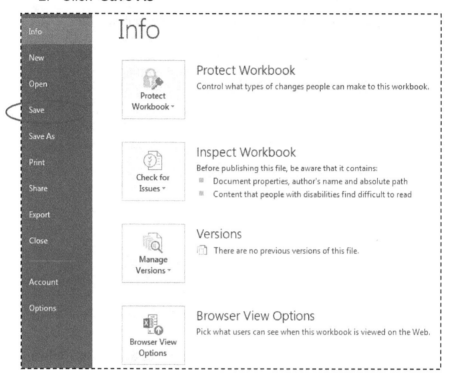

3. Select a location to save your file
4. When prompted, provide a file name
5. Click the **'Save'** button

CHAPTER 3
The Home Tab

The **'HOME'** tab contains commands for copying, cutting, pasting and formatting data. Some of the most often used commands are:

- Copy, Cut, & Paste
- Format Painter
- Font, Number, & Currency formatting
- Conditional Formatting

Copying, Cutting, & Pasting:

Excel® makes it easy to cut, copy, and paste data, allowing you to make changes quickly.

Copy

To **copy** the contents of one more cells, highlight the cells and click the 'Copy' button. You may also press **CTRL+C** on your keyboard.

Cut

To **cut** the contents of one more cells, highlight the cells and click the 'Cut' button. You may also press **CTRL+X** on your keyboard.

Paste

There are a number of **paste** options available after the contents of one more cells have been copied or cut.

The *main* paste options are:

Paste:

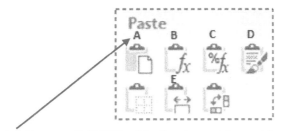

A. **Paste all (CTRL+V)**: Pastes all formatting and formulas

B. **Formulas only**: Pastes only formulas, no formatting

C. **Formulas & Number formatting**: Pastes only formulas and the *number* format

D. **Formatting only**: Pastes only the formatting, no values or formulas

E. **Keep source column widths**: Pastes the column width(s), all formulas, and formatting

Paste Values:

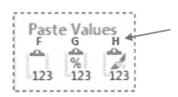

F. **Values Only**: This option appears only when the copied data contains formulas. It will paste only the value results, no formatting.

G. **Values and Number Formatting**: This option appears only when the copied data contains formulas. It will paste the value results and number formatting.

H. **Values and Source Formatting**: Removes all formulas (see 'Values Only') it will paste the value results and formatting.

Other Paste Options:

I.   **Link cells**: Links the pasted cells to their original location. For example, if you copy 'A1' to 'B1', cell 'B1' will contain a link to cell 'A1' (=A1), all formatting is removed.

Format Painter

'**Format Painter**' allows you to copy the formatting of a cell to one or more *other* cells. Click the Format Painter button on the cell that has the preferred format and then highlight the cells (with the paint brush) you want to copy the formatting to.

Font

There are several ways to change the font *style*, color, and shading of a cell, below are some examples:

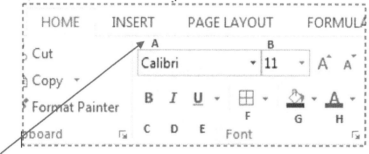

A. Font Style   *Click the drop-down box to select a different font style*
B. Font Size   Click to **increase** or decrease font size
C. **Bold**   Click to **bold** or press **CTRL+B** on your keyboard
D. *Italic*   Click to *italicize* or press **CTRL+I** on your keyboard
E. Underline   Click to Underline or press **CTRL+U** on your keyboard
F. Gridlines   Click to add or remove gridlines
G. Shading   Click to add or remove cell shading
H. Font Color Click to change the font color

Currency - *formatting*

There are several ways to change the format of a number to a currency value. The simplest, is to highlight the cells that have the numbers you want to change and click the $ (symbol) command. You may also use the adjoining commands to increase or decrease the number of decimal places.

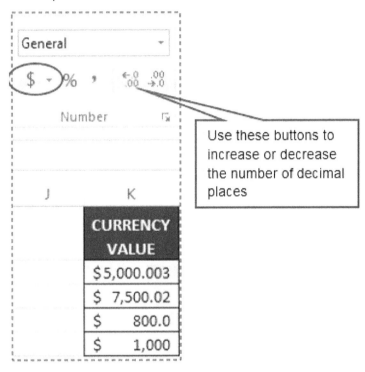

Use these buttons to increase or decrease the number of decimal places

CURRENCY VALUE
$5,000.003
$ 7,500.02
$ 800.0
$ 1,000

Below are two additional methods to change a currency symbol. In the following examples, I will demonstrate the **British Pound £** and **Euro €**:

1. Select the cells you would like to change the currency, in this example, cells 'B2' – 'B6' are highlighted:

	A	B	C
1	US	British Pound	Euro
2	$ 100	100	100
3	$ 200	200	200
4	$ 300	300	300
5	$ 400	400	400
6	$ 500	500	500

2. From the **'HOME'** toolbar click the drop-down box for **$**

3. Select one of the currency's listed, in this example, '**£ English (United Kingdom)**' was selected:

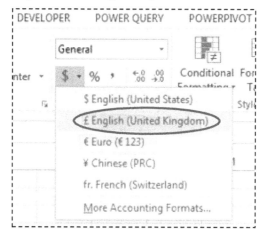

Alternatively, if your desired currency is not listed in the **'HOME'** ribbon tab **$** drop-down box, you can:

1. Select the cells you would like to change the currency
2. **Right click** and select **'Format Cells…'**:

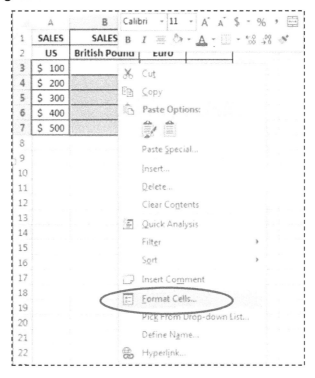

3. Select the tab **'Number'**

4. **'Category:' 'Currency'**

5. In the **'Symbol'** drop-down box select your desired currency, in this example, *'£ Engilsh (United Kingom)'* was selected:

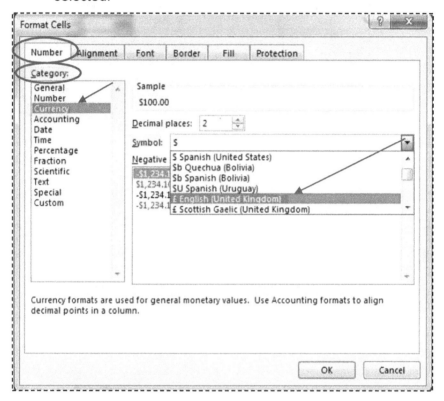

6. Click the **'OK'** button

Repeat the preferred method above, this time for the '**Euro €**' currency

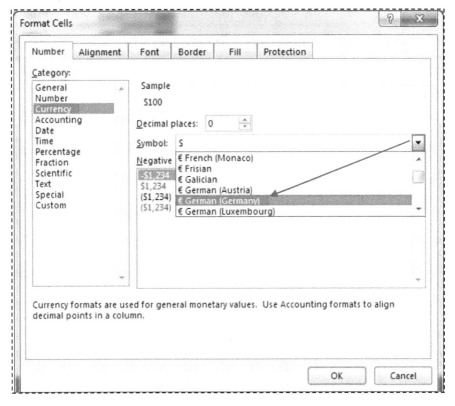

We now have currency displayed in the **British Pound £** and **Euro €**:

	A	B	C
1	US	British Pound	Euro
2	$ 100	£100	100 €
3	$ 200	£200	200 €
4	$ 300	£300	300 €
5	$ 400	£400	400 €
6	$ 500	£500	500 €

Number & Percent - *formatting*

To change a value to a *number format* or *percent* is similar to currency formatting. Highlight the cells that have the values you want to change and click the **number (,) or percent (%) symbol**. You may also use the adjoining commands to increase or decrease the decimal places.

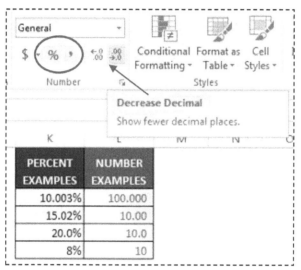

Conditional - *formatting*

Using different colors for cell shading and fonts, **Conditional Formatting** allows you to highlight cells based on *specific criteria*.

Some preset options include:
- The Top & Bottom 10 *(the **number** 10 can be adjusted)*
- The Top & Bottom 10% *(this **percentage** can also be adjusted)*
- Above & Below the Average

A very useful tool to quickly identify:
- Duplicate values
- A reoccurring date
- Values greater or less than a specific number
- Equal to a specific number
- Cells that contain specific text

Example:

In the below spreadsheet you want identify the duplicate names *(this feature is more useful with lots of records)*:

1. Highlight **column 'B'**
2. From the ribbon select **HOME > Conditional Formatting**

3. Select **Highlight Cells Rules > Duplicate Values**

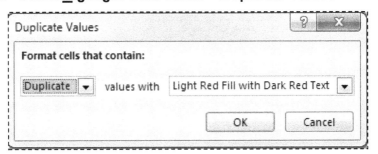

4. Select a shading option, such as '**Light Red Fill with Dark Red Text'**

5. Click the '**OK**' button

You have now identified the duplicate names:

	A	B	C
	SALES PERSON FIRST NAME	SALES PERSON LAST NAME	SALES
1			
2	Jack	Smith	$ 1,849
3	Joe	Tanner	$ 2,404
4	Peter	Graham	$ 3,125
5	Helen	Simpson	$ 4,062
6	Alex	Steller	$ 5,281
7	Billy	Winchester	$ 2,865
8	Jack	Smith	$ 1,849

CHAPTER 4
The Insert Tab

The **'INSERT'** tab contains commands for creating Pivot Tables and presentation tools such as graphing and illustrations. Some of the most often used commands are:

- PivotTable
- Charts
- Illustrations

Pivot Tables

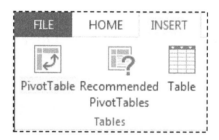

As your experience with Excel® grows, you'll likely start working with more and more data. Pivot Tables, allow you to quickly organize and summarize large amounts of information.

> **Pivot Tables** use built-in filters and functions to quickly organize, summarize, and filter large amounts of records.

Pivot Tables, which are discussed in further detail in chapter 14, provide a means for performing various types of analysis without needing to manually enter formulas into the spreadsheet you're analyzing. Pivot Tables save time and provide one of the easiest methods to perform ad hoc or dashboard reporting.

For example, you developed or were given a spreadsheet with several hundred rows and approximately ten columns of sales type data, such as sales by store, region, sales person, month, quarter etc. With just a few clicks you can create a sales summary report, such as the below:

SALES	MONTH ▾					
REGION ⊽	January	February	March	April	May	TOTAL
Central	$11,359	$19,352	$34,097	$73,763	$81,463	$220,034
East	$3,865	$19,343	$38,811	$83,569	$88,469	$234,057
West	$2,231	$18,472	$38,170	$110,704	$117,054	$286,631
TOTAL	$17,455	$57,168	$111,078	$268,036	$286,986	$740,723

For more examples of Pivot Table reports, please see chapter 14.

Charts

Similarly, as with Pivot Tables when you start working with more and more data, charting is another tool summarize information. Only instead of using tables, it summarizes and displays data graphically.

Example

If you wanted to quickly see how fruit sales were trending by month. Using the data from the following spreadsheet, you would simply:

Highlight columns **'A1' – 'C13'**

	A	B	C
1	MONTH	APPLES	ORANGES
2	January	£ 3,865	£ 1,739
3	February	£ 9,231	£ 4,154
4	March	£ 11,359	£ 5,112
5	April	£ 13,547	£ 19,352
6	May	£ 23,868	£ 34,097
7	June	£ 26,719	£ 38,170
8	July	£ 11,768	£ 16,811
9	August	£ 12,931	£ 18,472
10	September	£ 13,540	£ 19,343
11	October	£ 53,763	£ 24,193
12	November	£ 43,569	£ 19,606
13	December	£ 20,704	£ 9,317

Select the **'INSERT'** tab and **'Insert Line Chart',** in this example the **'Line with Marker'** graph is selected.

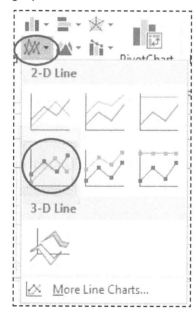

A chart similar to the following should now be displayed:

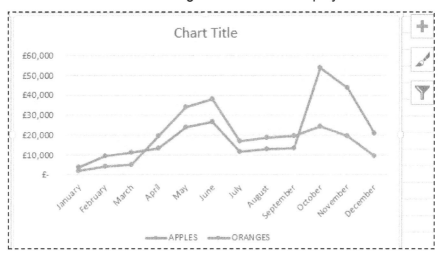

Illustrations

There may come a time when you would like to draw attention to specific details of your spreadsheet. To accomplish this you could use *arrows* or *callouts*, which are options available under

Illustrations:

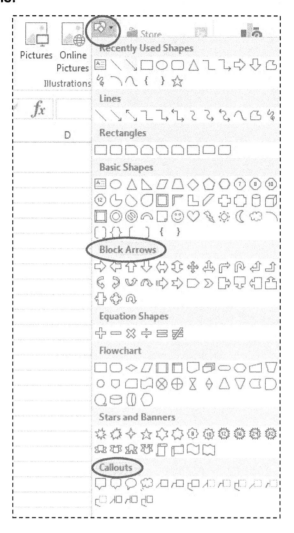

Below are two examples of how an **arrow** and **callout** illustration
can be applied to a worksheet:

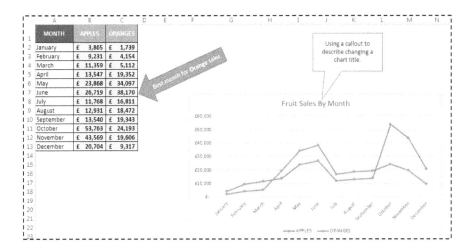

CHAPTER 5

The Page Layout Tab

The **'PAGE LAYOUT'** tab is one option where you can set and modify your print settings.

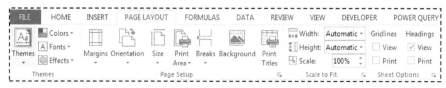

Print

Two quicks ways to preview your spreadsheet before printing or to change the print settings are:

1) Clicking the **'Print Preview'** icon, once added to your **'Quick Access Toolbar'** *(please see chapter 2 for instructions on how to add commands to the Quick Access Toolbar)*

2) Open *(by clicking the expand arrow)* the **'Page Setup'** section of the **'Page Layout'** tab.

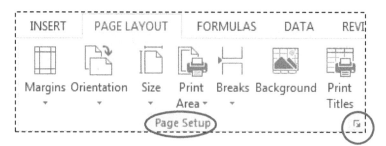

Let's walk through an example. I am attempting to print the following spreadsheet including the chart:

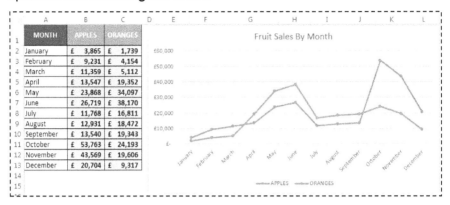

1. Open the **'Page Setup'** section of the **'Page Layout'** tab, by clicking the expand arrow

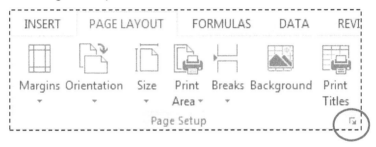

2. The following dialogue box will appear. Click the **'Print Preview'** button

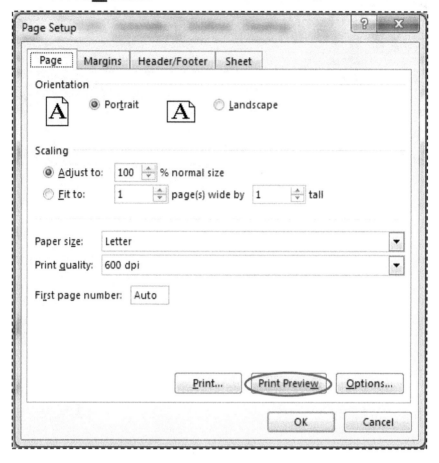

As you can see, the spreadsheet would print across two pages.

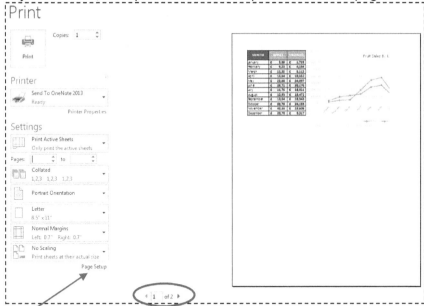

3. Select **'Page Setup'** button under **Settings**
4. Change the **'Orientation'** to **'Landscape'**
5. Change the **'Scaling'** to **'Fit to: 1'** and click the **'OK'** button

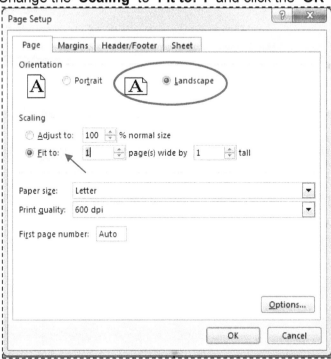

The following spreadsheet including the chart will now print on one page:

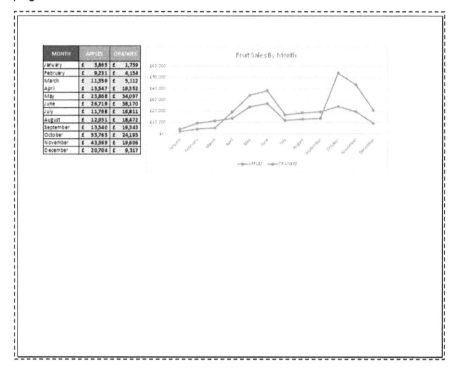

Additional print settings (Margins, Header, & Footer)

1. To **center** the contents, from the **'Page Setup'** dialogue box

2. Select the **'Margins'** tab

3. Select one or both '**Center on page**' check boxes

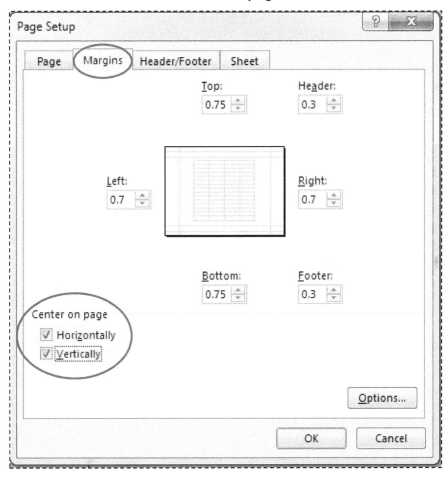

4. To add a **Header or Footer**, from the **'Page Setup'** dialogue box

5. Select the **'Header/Footer'** tab

6. Select a drop-down option for the either or both the **Header or Footer**

7. Click the '**OK**' button

Example of a spreadsheet with a **Header or Footer** added:

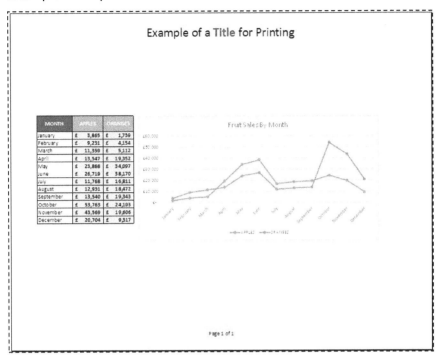

CHAPTER 6
The Data Tab

The **'DATA'** tab contains commands for importing, sorting, filtering, and grouping data. Some of the most often used commands are:

- Sort
- Filter
- Subtotal

Filter

The **'Filter'** command turns each column heading into a drop-down box in which you can apply filtering criteria.

Example:

The following spreadsheet contains fifty stores *(only 20 are displayed)*. By highlighting the header row (row 1) and clicking the

'Filter' button, I can now filter for specific stores or regions.

STORE	REGION	Q1 SALES	Q2 SALES	Q3 SALES	Q4 SALES
Store 111	East	£20,000	£ 20,277	£ 20,561	£ 20,950
Store 112	West	£21,000	£ 21,277	£ 21,561	£ 21,950
Store 113	Central	£22,000	£ 22,277	£ 22,561	£ 22,950
Store 114	East	£23,000	£ 23,277	£ 23,561	£ 23,950
Store 115	West	£24,000	£ 24,277	£ 24,561	£ 24,950
Store 116	Central	£25,000	£ 25,277	£ 25,561	£ 25,950
Store 117	East	£20,000	£ 30,000	£ 34,000	£ 40,000
Store 118	West	£21,000	£ 31,500	£ 35,700	£ 42,000
Store 119	Central	£22,000	£ 33,000	£ 37,400	£ 44,000
Store 120	East	£23,000	£ 34,500	£ 39,100	£ 46,000
Store 121	West	£24,000	£ 36,000	£ 40,800	£ 48,000
Store 122	Central	£25,000	£ 37,500	£ 42,500	£ 50,000
Store 123	East	£23,000	£ 23,277	£ 23,561	£ 23,950
Store 124	West	£24,000	£ 24,277	£ 24,561	£ 24,950
Store 125	Central	£25,000	£ 25,277	£ 25,561	£ 25,950
Store 126	East	£20,000	£ 20,277	£ 20,561	£ 20,950
Store 127	West	£21,000	£ 21,277	£ 21,561	£ 21,950
Store 128	Central	£25,000	£ 25,277	£ 25,561	£ 25,950
Store 129	East	£20,000	£ 30,000	£ 34,000	£ 40,000
Store 130	West	£21,000	£ 31,500	£ 35,700	£ 42,000

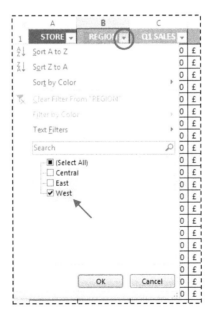

The spreadsheet is now filtered for the West region *(**note:** the other region rows are hidden):*

	A	B	C	D	E	F
1	STORE ▼	REGION 🔽	Q1 SALES ▼	Q2 SALES ▼	Q3 SALES ▼	Q4 SALES ▼
3	Store 112	West	£ 21,000	£ 21,277	£ 21,561	£ 21,950
6	Store 115	West	£ 24,000	£ 24,277	£ 24,561	£ 24,950
9	Store 118	West	£ 21,000	£ 31,500	£ 35,700	£ 42,000
12	Store 121	West	£ 24,000	£ 36,000	£ 40,800	£ 48,000
15	Store 124	West	£ 24,000	£ 24,277	£ 24,561	£ 24,950
18	Store 127	West	£ 21,000	£ 21,277	£ 21,561	£ 21,950
21	Store 130	West	£ 21,000	£ 31,500	£ 35,700	£ 42,000
24	Store 133	West	£ 24,000	£ 36,000	£ 40,800	£ 48,000
27	Store 136	West	£ 21,000	£ 21,277	£ 21,561	£ 21,950
30	Store 139	West	£ 24,000	£ 24,277	£ 24,561	£ 24,950
33	Store 142	West	£ 24,000	£ 36,000	£ 40,800	£ 48,000
36	Store 145	West	£ 21,000	£ 31,500	£ 35,700	£ 42,000
40	Store 149	West	£ 20,900	£ 21,177	£ 21,461	£ 21,850
43	Store 152	West	£ 19,800	£ 20,077	£ 20,361	£ 20,750
46	Store 155	West	£ 24,700	£ 37,050	£ 41,990	£ 49,400
49	Store 158	West	£ 24,700	£ 37,050	£ 41,990	£ 49,400

Sort

Sorting allows you to organize your data into a different order.

Example:

Using the same data as above, I will sort by region, then store number. First, I will highlight all of my data (including the header, row 1) and then click the **'Sort'** ⬓ button.

The following dialogue box will appear. I selected my primary and secondary sorting options and clicked the 'OK' button. *(**note:** the box for 'My data has headers' is checked)*

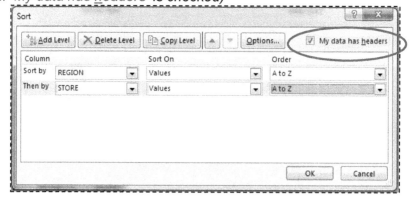

The spreadsheet is now sorted, by *region* then *store* number:

STORE	REGION	Q1 SALES	Q2 SALES	Q3 SALES	Q4 SALES
Store 113	Central	£ 22,000	£ 22,277	£ 22,561	£ 22,950
Store 116	Central	£ 25,000	£ 25,277	£ 25,561	£ 25,950
Store 119	Central	£ 22,000	£ 33,000	£ 37,400	£ 44,000
Store 122	Central	£ 25,000	£ 37,500	£ 42,500	£ 50,000
Store 125	Central	£ 25,000	£ 25,277	£ 25,561	£ 25,950
Store 128	Central	£ 25,000	£ 25,277	£ 25,561	£ 25,950
Store 131	Central	£ 22,000	£ 33,000	£ 37,400	£ 44,000
Store 134	Central	£ 25,000	£ 37,500	£ 42,500	£ 50,000
Store 137	Central	£ 22,000	£ 22,277	£ 22,561	£ 22,950
Store 140	Central	£ 25,000	£ 25,277	£ 25,561	£ 25,950
Store 143	Central	£ 25,000	£ 37,500	£ 42,500	£ 50,000
Store 146	Central	£ 25,000	£ 37,500	£ 42,500	£ 50,000
Store 147	Central	£ 21,900	£ 22,177	£ 22,461	£ 22,850
Store 150	Central	£ 24,900	£ 25,177	£ 25,461	£ 25,850
Store 153	Central	£ 24,900	£ 37,350	£ 42,330	£ 49,800
Store 156	Central	£ 24,900	£ 37,350	£ 42,330	£ 49,800
Store 159	Central	£ 21,800	£ 32,700	£ 37,060	£ 43,600
Store 111	East	£ 20,000	£ 20,277	£ 20,561	£ 20,950
Store 114	East	£ 23,000	£ 23,277	£ 23,561	£ 23,950
Store 117	East	£ 20,000	£ 30,000	£ 34,000	£ 40,000
Store 120	East	£ 23,000	£ 34,500	£ 39,100	£ 46,000
Store 123	East	£ 23,000	£ 23,277	£ 23,561	£ 23,950
Store 126	East	£ 20,000	£ 20,277	£ 20,561	£ 20,950

Subtotal

The subtotal command allows you add subtotaling formulas to your spreadsheet based on criteria you specify. *Your spreadsheet must contain numeric data to use the feature.*

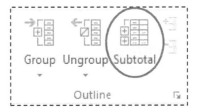

Example:

Using the same data as above, I will subtotal quarterly sales by region.

1. Highlight all the records (including the header row)

2. Click the **'Subtotal'** button. *(**note:** your data needs to first be sorted in a group order, i.e. region)*

The following dialogue box will appear. I selected the appropriate subtotaling criteria and clicked the '**OK**' button:

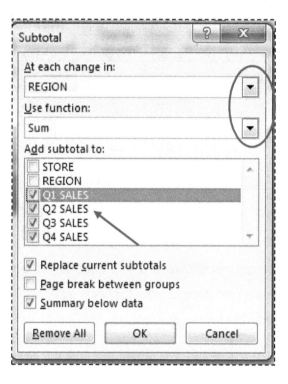

The following subtotal rows have been added to the spreadsheet (***note:*** *the group buttons in the right margin):*

	STORE	REGION	Q1 SALES	Q2 SALES	Q3 SALES	Q4 SALES
1	STORE	REGION	Q1 SALES	Q2 SALES	Q3 SALES	Q4 SALES
2	Store 113	Central	£ 22,000	£ 22,277	£ 22,561	£ 22,950
3	Store 116	Central	£ 25,000	£ 25,277	£ 25,561	£ 25,950
4	Store 119	Central	£ 22,000	£ 33,000	£ 37,400	£ 44,000
5	Store 122	Central	£ 25,000	£ 37,500	£ 42,500	£ 50,000
6	Store 125	Central	£ 25,000	£ 25,277	£ 25,561	£ 25,950
7	Store 128	Central	£ 25,000	£ 25,277	£ 25,561	£ 25,950
8	Store 131	Central	£ 22,000	£ 33,000	£ 37,400	£ 44,000
9	Store 134	Central	£ 25,000	£ 37,500	£ 42,500	£ 50,000
10	Store 137	Central	£ 22,000	£ 22,277	£ 22,561	£ 22,950
11	Store 140	Central	£ 25,000	£ 25,277	£ 25,561	£ 25,950
12	Store 143	Central	£ 25,000	£ 37,500	£ 42,500	£ 50,000
13	Store 146	Central	£ 25,000	£ 37,500	£ 42,500	£ 50,000
14	Store 147	Central	£ 21,900	£ 22,177	£ 22,461	£ 22,850
15	Store 150	Central	£ 24,900	£ 25,177	£ 25,461	£ 25,850
16	Store 153	Central	£ 24,900	£ 37,350	£ 42,330	£ 49,800
17	Store 156	Central	£ 24,900	£ 37,350	£ 42,330	£ 49,800
18	Store 159	Central	£ 21,800	£ 32,700	£ 37,060	£ 43,600
19		Central Total	£ 406,400	£ 516,416	£ 561,808	£ 629,600

Example of regions subtotaled and grouped (level 2):

	STORE	REGION	Q1 SALES	Q2 SALES	Q3 SALES	Q4 SALES
1	STORE	REGION	Q1 SALES	Q2 SALES	Q3 SALES	Q4 SALES
19		Central Total	£ 406,400	£ 516,416	£ 561,808	£ 629,600
37		East Total	£ 363,400	£ 461,416	£ 502,008	£ 562,600
54		West Total	£ 359,600	£ 451,716	£ 489,948	£ 547,000
55		Grand Total	£ 1,129,400	£ 1,429,548	£ 1,553,764	£ 1,739,200

Example with the West region ungrouped (expanded):

	STORE	REGION	Q1 SALES	Q2 SALES	Q3 SALES	Q4 SALES
19		Central Total	£ 406,400	£ 516,416	£ 561,808	£ 629,600
37		East Total	£ 363,400	£ 461,416	£ 502,008	£ 562,600
38	Store 112	West	£ 21,000	£ 21,277	£ 21,561	£ 21,950
39	Store 115	West	£ 24,000	£ 24,277	£ 24,561	£ 24,950
40	Store 118	West	£ 21,000	£ 31,500	£ 35,700	£ 42,000
41	Store 121	West	£ 24,000	£ 36,000	£ 40,800	£ 48,000
42	Store 124	West	£ 24,000	£ 24,277	£ 24,561	£ 24,950
43	Store 127	West	£ 21,000	£ 21,277	£ 21,561	£ 21,950
44	Store 130	West	£ 21,000	£ 31,500	£ 35,700	£ 42,000
45	Store 133	West	£ 24,000	£ 36,000	£ 40,800	£ 48,000
46	Store 136	West	£ 21,000	£ 21,277	£ 21,561	£ 21,950
47	Store 139	West	£ 24,000	£ 24,277	£ 24,561	£ 24,950
48	Store 142	West	£ 24,000	£ 36,000	£ 40,800	£ 48,000
49	Store 145	West	£ 21,000	£ 31,500	£ 35,700	£ 42,000
50	Store 149	West	£ 20,900	£ 21,177	£ 21,461	£ 21,850
51	Store 152	West	£ 23,900	£ 24,177	£ 24,461	£ 24,850
52	Store 155	West	£ 23,900	£ 35,850	£ 40,630	£ 47,800
53	Store 158	West	£ 20,900	£ 31,350	£ 35,530	£ 41,800
54		West Total	£ 359,600	£ 451,716	£ 489,948	£ 547,000
55		Grand Total	£ 1,129,400	£ 1,429,548	£ 1,553,764	£ 1,739,200

CHAPTER 7

The Review Tab

The **'REVIEW'** tab contains commands for proofing and protecting your worksheets and workbooks. Some of the most often used commands:

- Spellcheck & Thesaurus
- Protecting worksheets & workbooks

Spellcheck & Thesaurus

To check the spelling of text content in your worksheet, click the **'Spelling'** command or press **F7** on your keyboard.

To access the Thesaurus click the **'Thesaurus'** command or press **Shift+F7** on your keyboard.

Protecting worksheets & workbooks

To avoid someone or yourself from accidentally deleting or changing content (including formulas), you can protect the worksheet(s) within a workbook or the workbook file itself.

To protect the workbook, select the **'Protect Workbook'** command and enter a password or leave blank.

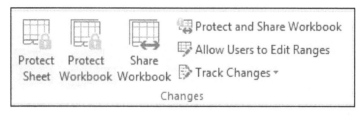

To protect the worksheet:

1. Select the **'Protect Sheet'** command

The following dialogue box will appear:

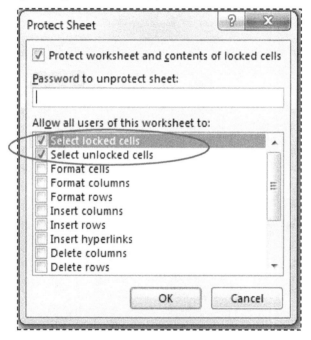

2. You may enter a password or leave blank
3. A good best practice is to leave the first two check boxes selected *(these will allow you to click on cells and scroll, but not change any content):*
   a. Select locked cells
   b. Select unlocked cells
4. Click the **'OK'** button

If someone tries to modify the sheet, they will receive the following message:

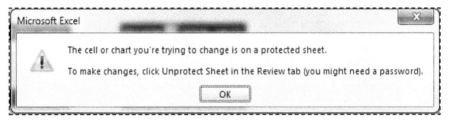

To **unprotect**, select **'Unprotect Sheet...'** *(this option will become available if a sheet is protected)*

CHAPTER 8

The View Tab

Some of the frequently used commands of the **'VIEW'** tab are:

- Freeze Panes
- Split (screen)

Freeze Panes

'Freeze Panes' keeps the column and rows that you specify locked when scrolling down and to the left. When working with large amounts of information, for example spreadsheets with more than a fifty rows and five-seven columns of data, **'Freeze Panes'** is a very helpful command. You may even add this command to your **'Quick Access Toolbar'** *(please see chapter 2 for instructions on how to add commands to the Quick Access Toolbar)*.

> *Example*
> When scrolling to row 205, I can no longer see the column headings or the record number *(labeled in column 'A')* for this row:

	B	C	D	E	F	G	H	I
205	204	204.25	204.5	204.75	205	205.25	205.5	205.75
206	205	205.25	205.5	205.75	206	206.25	206.5	206.75
207	206	206.25	206.5	206.75	207	207.25	207.5	207.75
208	207	207.25	207.5	207.75	208	208.25	208.5	208.75

After applying the **'Freeze Panes'** command to cell **'B2'**:

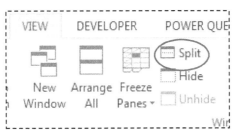

I can now see the column headings and the record number for this row when scrolling down and to the left:

	A	C	D	E	F	G	H	I
1	RECORD	HEADING 2	HEADING 3	HEADING 4	HEADING 5	HEADING 6	HEADING 7	HEADING 8
205	Record 314	204.25	204.5	204.75	205	205.25	205.5	205.75
206	Record 315	205.25	205.5	205.75	206	206.25	206.5	206.75
207	Record 316	206.25	206.5	206.75	207	207.25	207.5	207.75
208	Record 317	207.25	207.5	207.75	208	208.25	208.5	208.75

Split (screen)

Similarly, when working with large amounts data, if you wanted to analyze two records that were not close in order you could apply the **'Split'** command.

Example:

After applying the **'Split'** command to row 206. I can now compare two records that are not close in order:

205	Record 314	204	204.25	204.5	204.75	205	205.25	205.5	205.75
206	Record 315	205	205.25	205.5	205.75	206	206.25	206.5	206.75
1035	Record 1144	1034	1034.25	1034.5	1034.75	1035	1035.25	1035.5	1035.75
1036	Record 1145	1035	1035.25	1035.5	1035.75	1036	1036.25	1036.5	1036.75

CHAPTER 9

Basic Formulas (Part 1)

Sum, Subtraction, Multiplication, & Division

Excel® can perform simple calculations to very complex expression evaluations. In Excel®, calculations are entered into a cell in the structure of a **formula** or **function** and require the appropriate **syntax**.

Formula

> A **formula** calculates numbers or evaluates the contents of one or more cells.

Syntax

> **Syntax** in Excel® refers to the arrangement or order of a formula or function. All formulas & functions begin with the equal sign (=) followed by numbers or the function's name.

Function

> A **function** in Excel® is a predefined formula. An example of a function name is 'Count'.

In Excel®, the terms *'formula'* and *'function'* are used interchangeably, most users do not differentiate between the two. Even Microsoft® labels the tab 'FORMULA' when really it is more representative of functions. **From a teaching or conversational perspective, it is much easier to say *'formula',* because this is what most people are familiar with. Therefore, in this book, the term *'formula'* and not *'function'* is used more often.** I know, it can be a little confusing, but basically the subtle difference is, a 'function' is entered with a *name*, some examples are *Sum*, *Average*, and *Count* and typically involve the evaluation of other cells. A 'formula' can be entered with an operator like (+, -, * or /) and does not have to involve other cells. Here a two examples:

```
Formula:  =2+2          result is 4
Function: =SUM(B2:C2)   result is 4
```

In the proceeding chapters, **'formula'** is the term used for instruction.

Below are the fundamental formulas users typically learn first.

ARITHMETIC APPLICATION	OPERATOR	DEFINITION
Sum (addition)	+	Adds two or more cells or numbers together
Subtraction	-	Subtracts two or more cells or numbers
Multiplication	*	Multiplies two or more cells or numbers
Division	/	Divides two or more cells or numbers

Below is an example of how to enter a basic formula:

SUM

Begin by creating a new blank Excel® spreadsheet

1. Enter the following numbers into **column 'A'**
   a. Cell '**A1**' enter the number **2**
   b. Cell '**A2**' enter the number **3**
   c. Cell '**A3**' enter the number **1**
   d. Cell '**A4**' enter the number **2**

The spreadsheet should look similar to the following:

	A
1	2
2	3
3	1
4	2
5	

2. Click cell 'A5'

3. From the ribbon select **'FORMULAS'**

4. Click the Σ AutoSum (drop-down box)

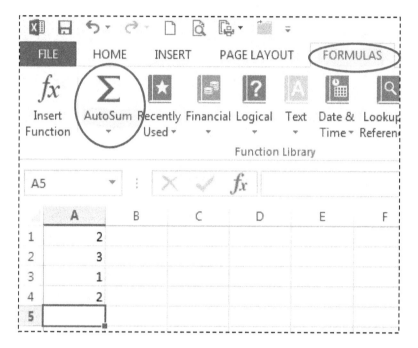

The result should be **8**:

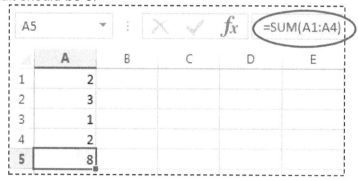

Alternatively, you may also enter the following into cell **'A5'**:

1. Enter the **equal (=)** $\boxed{\substack{+\\=}}$ symbol from your keyboard

2. Type **sum(**

3. Highlight rows **'A1-A4'**

4. Press the **'Enter'** $\boxed{\substack{\text{Enter}\\\leftarrow}}$ button on your keyboard

ADDITIONAL EXAMPLES:

	A	B	C	D	E
1	ARITHMETIC APPLICATION	EXAMPLE DATA	EXAMPLE DATA	FORMULA	RESULT
2	Sum	2	3	=SUM(B2:C2)	5
3	Sum	-	-	=SUM(2+3)	5
4	Sum	-	-	=2+3	5
6	Subtraction	3	1	=B6-C6	2
7	Subtraction	-	-	=3-1	2
9	Multiplication	7	9	=B9*C9	63
10	Multiplication	-	-	=7*9	63
12	Division	4	2	=B12/C12	2
13	Division	-	-	=4/2	2

	A	B	C	D
1	ADDING NUMBERS TOGETHER	SUM & MULTIPLICATION	SUM & DIVISION	
2	2	2	2	
3	3	3	3	
4	7	7	7	
5	4	4	4	
6	=A2+A3+A4+A5	=SUM(B2:B5)*2	=SUM(C2:C5)/2	FORMULA
7	16	32	8	RESULT

CHAPTER 10

Basic Formulas (Part 2)
Average, Min, Max, & Count

Once you're comfortable with the fundamental formulas, some additional formulas to learn are:

ARITHMETIC APPLICATION	FORMULA / FUNCTION	DEFINITION
Average	Average	Returns the **average number** in a range of values, does not include text in the evaluation
Minimum	Min	Returns the *lowest number* in a range of values, does not include text in the evaluation.
Maximum	Max	Returns the *largest number* in a range of values, does not include text in the evaluation.
Count	Count	**Counts** the number of cells that contain numbers in a range of values, does not include text in the evaluation

EXAMPLES:

The below examples are evaluating multiple cells:

	A	B	C	D	E
1	EXAMPLE DATA	EXAMPLE DATA	EXAMPLE DATA	EXAMPLE DATA	
2	100	2	3	1	
3	200	3	1	1	
4	300	7	9	2	
5	400	4	2	2	
6	=AVERAGE(A2:A5)	=MIN(B2:B5)	=MAX(C2:C5)	=COUNT(D2:D5)	FORMULA
7	250	2	9	4	RESULTS

ADDITIONAL EXAMPLES:

FORMULA	RESULT
=AVERAGE(200, 300, 200, 300)	250
=MIN(1,2,3,4)	1
=MAX(1,2,3,4)	4

CHAPTER 11

Date Formulas

Today, Now, & Networkdays

Below are the most commonly used date and time formulas.

FORMULA	DEFINITION
Today	Provides today's date. **NOTE**: this formula will update each day, it is always the current date.
Now	Returns the current date *and* time. **NOTE**: this formula will update each day, it is always the current date *and* time of when the spreadsheet is opened.
Networkdays	Calculates the number of **workdays** (Monday – Friday) between two dates.

EXAMPLES:

TODAY & NOW:

	A	B
1	**FORMULA**	**RESULT**
2	=TODAY()	7/13/2015
3	=NOW()	7/13/2015 10:28 AM

NETWORKDAYS:

C2	▼	:	✕	✓	*fx*	=NETWORKDAYS(A2,B2)

	A	B	C	D	E
1	**START DATE**	**COMPLETION DATE**	**HOW MANY WORKDAYS?**		
2	8/1/2015	10/31/2015	65		
3					

You may also change the *format* of dates, below are some examples.

FROM:	TO:	
11/18/2015	Wednesday, November 18, 2015	Includes weekday
11/18/2015	November 18, 2015	Month spelled out
11/18/2015	18-Nov-2015	International
11/18/2015	18/11/2015	British United Kingdom
11/18/2015	18. Nov. 2015	German

1. To change, from the ribbon select **HOME** : **Number**
2. Click the expand arrow

3. The **'Format Cells'** dialogue box will appear:

4. Select the **'Number'** tab

5. **'Date'** as the category

6. In the **'Type:'** box select your preferred format

7. Select a **'Locale (location):'** *if applicable*

8. Click the **'OK'** button

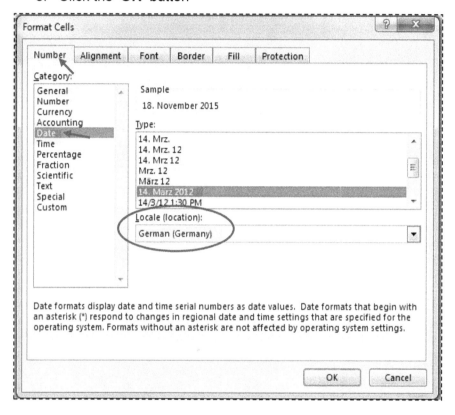

CHAPTER 12

Informational Formulas

Cell & Sheets

These formulas are very useful when you're working with a workbook with a large number of tabs or need the full file location path for use in a hyperlink or documentation.

FORMULA	DEFINITION
Cell (filename)	Returns the full file location path of the active workbook
Sheets	Provides the total number of sheets in the active workbook

EXAMPLES:

CELL (filename)
Returns the path of the file location:

FORMULA:	RESULT:
=CELL("filename")	C:\Users\CBenton\Documents\Books\[StartHere.xlsx]Chapter8

SHEETS
Counts the total number of sheets in a workbook:

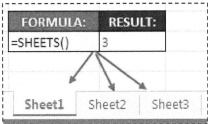

FORMULA:	RESULT:
=SHEETS()	3

| Sheet1 | Sheet2 | Sheet3 |

CHAPTER 13

The Formulas Tab

As the name implies the **'Formula'** tab is all about formulas, it contains commands for inserting a formula, the function library, and formula auditing. Some of the most often used commands are:

- Insert Function
- AutoSum
- Function Library
- Trace Precedents

Insert Function

Think of **'Insert Function'** as a guide, that provides the correct syntax for a specific formula.

CountIF Example

> Let's say you wanted to determine the number of stores that had sales greater than £10,000. You surmised **CountIF** was an appropriate formula, but weren't sure what the correct syntax was. This is where **'Insert Function'** becomes very helpful.

1. In cell **'B7'** click the **'Insert Function'** command from the **'FORMULAS'** tab or the function symbol near the formula bar

The following dialogue box will appear:

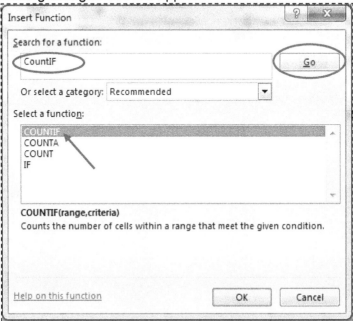

2. In the **'Search for function'** box type **CountIF**

3. Click the **'GO'** button

4. Verify COUNTIF is selected in the **'Select a function'** box

5. Click the **'OK'** button

The following **'Function Arguments'** dialogue box will appear:

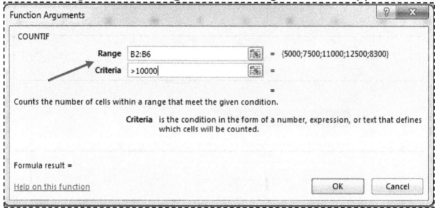

6. Enter the appropriate **'Range'** and **'Criteria'**

7. Click the **'OK'** button

	A	B	C	D	E	F
	B7	fx	=COUNTIF(B2:B6,">10000")			
1	STORE #	SALES				
2	Store 1	£5,000				
3	Store 2	£7,500				
4	Store 3	£11,000				
5	Store 4	£12,500				
6	Store 5	£8,300				
7	Stores > £10,000	2				

∑ AutoSum

AutoSum is part of the Function Library and is used to quickly apply the Sum, Average, Count, Min, & Max formulas to a cell.

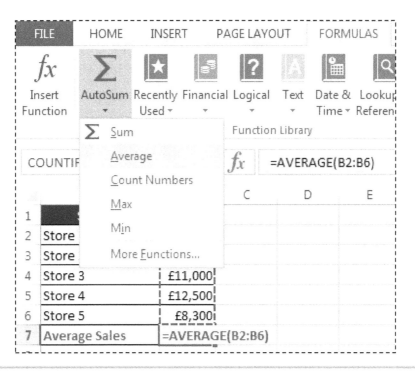

Function Library

Excel® has hundreds of formulas, the **'Function Library'** is a great way to learn about them. After you click a library drop-down box, you can place your cursor next to a function name and get a brief description as to what that formula does. If you click on the function

name, Excel® will lunch the **'Function Arguments'** dialogue box for
that formula.

Function Library:

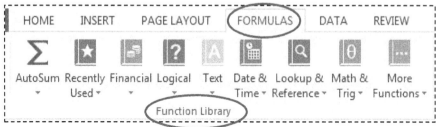

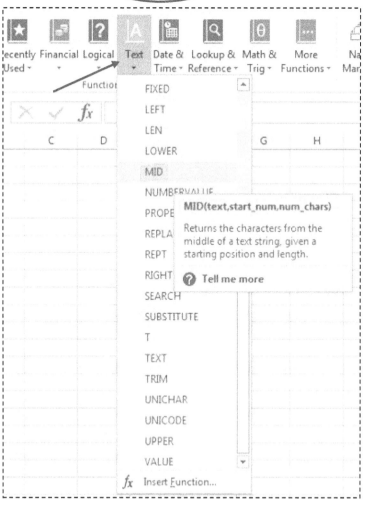

Trace Precedents

Trace Precedents is a **'Formula Auditing'** command. It will display graphically, with blue arrows, all of the cells a formula is referencing. A very useful feature when you need to troubleshoot or validate a formula is calculating correctly, especially when troubleshooting complex formulas or functions referencing many cells.

Example:

The formula in cell **'B3'** is *referencing values* in **cells 'A2', 'A4', & 'A5'**:

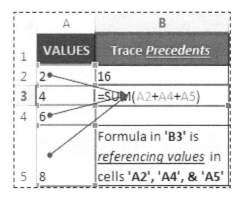

CHAPTER 14

Next Steps - An Introduction To Excel® Intermediate Formulas & Features

I hope the previous chapters have provided you with a solid overview of the basics of Excel®.

This chapter will introduce some intermediate level formulas and features. **While the below <u>is not a comprehensive</u> list of *all* the intermediate functionality available in Microsoft® Excel®, <u>nor is it intended to be a "how-to" guide</u>**, I hope it demonstrates a little more the power of Excel®. Let's take a closer look at some examples of:

- Data Validation
- Pivot Tables
- The VLOOKUP formula
- IF & NESTED formulas

DATA VALIDATION

Data validation is a way to create a **drop-down box** list of values that can be entered into a cell. It effectively limits what is considered a *valid value* for a specific cell. For example, you wanted to limit how a user entered a month value into a form. To improve efficiency, consistency, and reduce typing errors, you could use **data validation** to restrict the month entry to the three letter abbreviation (please see screenshot below).

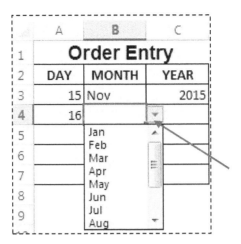

A few more examples of how data validation can be used:

- **To limit numbers outside a specified range:** For example, you can specify a maximum bonus of 1% based on sales number in a particular cell.

- **To limit dates outside a certain time frame:** For example, a date cannot be more than 365 days from today's date.

PIVOT TABLES

While Pivot Tables were introduced in chapter 4, I wanted to expand on this feature, because it exemplifies Excel's® capabilities for analysis.

As described in chapter 4, Pivot Tables allow you to quickly organize, summarize, and filter large amounts of data. However, with Pivot Tables you can also:

- Display averages & percentages
- Group data into predefined ranges
- Summarize individual dates into months and years
- Rank results
- Insert calculated fields

Let's say you were tasked with assessing significant amounts of data, perhaps consisting of several thousand or hundreds of thousands of records. Or, you may have to reconcile information from many different sources and forms, such as assimilating material from:

1. Reports generated by another application, such as a legacy system
2. Data imported into Excel® via a query from a database or other application
3. Data copied or cut, and pasted into Excel® from the web or other types of screen scraping activities

One of the easiest ways to perform high level analysis on this information is to use Pivot Tables. Below are some of the types of reporting that can be done with Pivot Tables.

Summarize and organize records:

For the first example, let's say you have list of records like the below, with just a few clicks, you can create summaries such as:

- The total sales by region and quarter
- The individual fruit sales by region and quarter
- Identify what the percentage of individual fruit sales are by quarter
- Rank each sales person, including their total & average sales

	A	B	C	D	E	F	G	H	I
1	REGION	SALES PERSON FIRST NAME	SALES PERSON LAST NAME	SALES PERSON ID	QUARTER	APPLES	ORANGES	MANGOS	TOTAL
2	Central	bob	TAYLOR	1174	1	1,810	2,039	1,771	5,620
3	Central	helen	SMITH	833	1	102	354	59	516
4	Central	jill	JOHNSON	200	1	93	322	54	469
5	Central	sally	MORTON	500	1	595	824	556	1,975
6	Central	sam	BECKER	800	1	863	1,092	824	2,779
7	East	Abbey	Williams	690	1	346	237	260	843
8	East	John	Dower	255	1	260	178	195	633
9	East	John	Wilson	300	1	286	196	215	696
10	East	Mary	Nelson	600	1	315	215	236	766
11	East	Sarah	Taylor	900	1	381	261	285	927
12	West	Alex	Steller	1000	1	163	212	127	502
13	West	Billy	Winchester	1156	1	179	234	140	552
14	West	Helen	Simpson	817	1	148	193	116	457
15	West	Jack	Smith	100	1	111	145	87	343
16	West	Joe	Tanner	400	1	122	160	96	377
17	West	Peter	Graham	700	1	134	175	105	415
18	Central	bob	TAYLOR	1174	2	113	390	65	567
19	Central	helen	SMITH	833	2	1,006	1,393	940	3,338
20	Central	jill	JOHNSON	200	2	774	1,071	723	2,568
21	Central	sally	MORTON	500	2	1,295	1,638	1,236	4,169
22	Central	sam	BECKER	800	2	2,806	3,160	2,745	8,711
23	East	Abbey	Williams	690	2	1,674	1,494	1,531	4,699
24	East	John	Dower	255	2	762	680	697	2,139
25	East	John	Wilson	300	2	991	884	906	2,781
26	East	Mary	Nelson	600	2	1,288	1,149	1,178	3,615
27	East	Sarah	Taylor	900	2	2,176	1,942	1,991	6,109
28	West	Alex	Steller	1000	2	1,751	1,848	1,682	5,281
29	West	Billy	Winchester	1156	2	2,276	2,402	2,187	6,865
30	West	Helen	Simpson	817	2	1,347	1,421	1,294	4,062

Due to space limitations, the entire dataset is not displayed:

	A	B	C	D	E	F	G	H	I
45	West	Billy	Winchester	1156	3	6,690	5,095	4,772	16,558
46	West	Jack	Smith	100	3	881	915	857	2,653
47	West	Joe	Tanner	400	3	1,322	1,373	1,286	3,980
48	West	Peter	Graham	700	3	1,982	2,059	1,928	5,969
49	Central	bob	TAYLOR	1174	4	4,369	5,528	4,172	14,069
50	Central	helen	SMITH	833	4	10,447	11,769	10,222	32,439
51	Central	jill	JOHNSON	200	4	6,740	7,593	6,595	20,928
52	Central	sally	MORTON	500	4	136	471	79	687
53	Central	sam	BECKER	800	4	1,699	2,353	1,588	5,641
54	East	Abbey	Williams	690	4	7,362	7,057	7,120	21,539
55	East	John	Dower	255	4	1,977	1,895	1,912	5,784
56	East	John	Wilson	300	4	3,064	2,937	2,964	8,965
57	East	Mary	Nelson	600	4	4,750	4,553	4,594	13,896
58	East	Sarah	Taylor	900	4	11,411	10,938	11,036	33,385
59	West	Alex	Steller	1000	4	10,551	10,747	10,413	31,711
60	West	Billy	Winchester	1156	4	16,354	11,822	11,454	39,631
61	West	Helen	Simpson	817	4	2,973	3,088	2,892	8,954
62	West	Helen	Simpson	817	4	6,807	6,934	6,718	20,459
63	West	Jack	Smith	100	4	1,828	1,862	1,804	5,494
64	West	Joe	Tanner	400	4	2,833	2,886	2,796	8,516
65	West	Peter	Graham	700	4	4,392	4,473	4,334	13,199

Formatted example of *the total sales by region and quarter*, using the Microsoft® Excel® Pivot Tables feature:

	TOTALS SALES	BY QUARTER ▾				
4	REGION ▾	QTR 1	QTR 2	QTR 3	QTR 4	Grand Total
5	Central	$ 11,359	$19,352	$ 34,097	$ 73,763	$ 138,571
6	East	$ 3,865	$19,343	$ 38,811	$ 83,569	$ 145,588
7	West	$ 2,646	$23,586	$ 42,590	$127,964	$ 196,787
8	Grand Total	$ 17,870	$62,281	$115,499	$285,296	$ 480,946

Formatted example of *the individual fruit sales by region and quarter*, using the Microsoft® Excel® Pivot Tables feature:

	A REGION ▾	B TOTAL APPLES	C TOTAL ORANGES	D TOTAL MANGOS	E TOTAL SALES
4	⊟Central	$ 43,481	$ 53,278	$ 41,812	$ 138,571
5	QTR 1	$ 3,463	$ 4,631	$ 3,264	$ 11,359
6	QTR 2	$ 5,992	$ 7,652	$ 5,709	$ 19,352
7	QTR 3	$ 10,634	$ 13,280	$ 10,183	$ 34,097
8	QTR 4	$ 23,392	$ 27,715	$ 22,656	$ 73,763
9	⊟East	$ 50,626	$ 47,117	$ 47,845	$ 145,588
10	QTR 1	$ 1,587	$ 1,087	$ 1,190	$ 3,865
11	QTR 2	$ 6,891	$ 6,149	$ 6,303	$ 19,343
12	QTR 3	$ 13,583	$ 12,502	$ 12,726	$ 38,811
13	QTR 4	$ 28,564	$ 27,380	$ 27,625	$ 83,569
14	⊟West	$ 69,750	$ 65,259	$ 61,778	$ 196,787
15	QTR 1	$ 856	$ 1,119	$ 671	$ 2,646
16	QTR 2	$ 7,819	$ 8,253	$ 7,513	$ 23,586
17	QTR 3	$ 15,335	$ 14,074	$ 13,182	$ 42,590
18	QTR 4	$ 45,739	$ 41,813	$ 40,411	$ 127,964
19	Grand Total	$ 163,857	$ 165,655	$ 151,435	$ 480,946

Formatted example of *the percentage of individual fruit sales by quarter*, using the Microsoft® Excel® Pivot Tables feature:

3	QUARTER ▾	% of APPLES	% of ORANGES	% of MANGOS
4	QTR 1	4%	4%	3%
5	QTR 2	13%	13%	13%
6	QTR 3	24%	24%	24%
7	QTR 4	60%	59%	60%
8	Grand Total	100%	100%	100%

Please note: In Excel®, often the percentages when summed together may exceed or not equal 100%, this is due to Excel® rounding the percentages either up or down.

Formatted example of *ranking each sales person's performance, including their total & average sales*, using the Microsoft® Excel® Pivot Tables feature:

3	SALES PERSON ID ▾	TOTAL SALES	AVERAGE SALES	RANK
4	1156	$ 63,606	$ 15,902	1
5	900	$ 55,320	$ 13,830	2
6	1000	$ 50,925	$ 12,731	3
7	833	$ 45,671	$ 11,418	4
8	690	$ 37,013	$ 9,253	5
9	817	$ 33,932	$ 8,483	6
10	200	$ 30,217	$ 7,554	7
11	600	$ 24,899	$ 6,225	8
12	1174	$ 24,595	$ 6,149	9
13	700	$ 22,708	$ 5,677	10
14	500	$ 20,332	$ 5,083	11
15	800	$ 17,755	$ 4,439	12
16	300	$ 16,857	$ 4,214	13
17	400	$ 15,276	$ 3,819	14
18	255	$ 11,499	$ 2,875	15
19	100	$ 10,339	$ 2,585	16
20	Grand Total	$ 480,946	$ 7,515	

PIVOT TABLES (a few more examples):

Below are two examples of an advanced Pivot Table feature called **'Grouping'**. When you have a lot of detailed individual records such as customer demographics, sales, location data, dates, etc., Sometimes more insight can be gained when you can cluster this data into categories or ranges. The Pivot Table **'Grouping'** feature allows you to complete this type of segmented analysis.

Example of **'Grouping'** *individual dates into months.*

Sample data, due to space limitations **the entire dataset is not displayed**:

	A Order Date	B AMOUNT PURCHASED
1		
2	01/01/14	$ 142
3	01/02/14	$ 153
4	01/03/14	$ 442
5	01/04/14	$ 409
6	01/05/14	$ 136
7	01/06/14	$ 147
8	01/07/14	$ 436
9	01/08/14	$ 403
10	01/09/14	$ 1,500
11	01/10/14	$ 106
23	03/16/15	$ 277
24	03/17/15	$ 385
25	03/18/15	$ 533
30	03/23/15	$ 985
31	03/24/15	$ 752

Formatted results after using the Pivot Table **'Grouping'** feature:

YEAR & MONTH ▼	AMT PURCHASED
⊟ 2014	
Jan	£ 3,874
⊟ 2015	
Feb	£ 8,393
Mar	£ 4,590
TOTAL	£ 16,857

Example of **'Grouping'** the number of customers by how much they spent, with their segment's percentage to the overall sales total.

Sample data, *due to space limitations **the entire dataset is not displayed***:

	A CUSTOMER ID	B AMOUNT PURCHASED
1		
2	111	$ 142
3	222	$ 153
4	333	$ 442
5	444	$ 409
6	555	$ 136
7	666	$ 147
8	777	$ 436
9	888	$ 403
10	999	$ 1,500
11	1110	$ 106
12	1221	$ 395
22	2331	$ 100
23	2442	$ 277
24	2553	$ 385
25	2664	$ 533
26	2775	$ 100
27	2886	$ 401
28	2997	$ 400
29	3108	$ 657
30	3219	$ 985
31	3330	$ 752

Formatted results after using the Pivot Table **'Grouping'** feature:

	AMOUNT PURCHASED ▾	NUMBER OF CUSTOMERS	% OF CUSTOMERS
4	100-199	7	23%
5	200-299	1	3%
6	300-399	3	10%
7	400-499	6	20%
8	500-599	1	3%
9	600-699	1	3%
10	700-799	3	10%
11	800-899	2	7%
12	900-999	1	3%
13	1000-1099	2	7%
14	1100-1199	2	7%
15	1400-1500	1	3%
16	**Grand Total**	30	100%

These are just few examples of the Pivot Table functionality:

If you would like to learn more about Pivot Tables, please check out my book: The Step-By-Step Guide To Pivot Tables & Introduction To Dashboards

The book contains several basic, intermediate, and advanced **step-by-step** Pivot Table examples with screenshots demonstrating how to:
- Organize and summarize data
- Format results
- Inserting both bar and pie Pivot Charts
- Displaying averages & percentages
- Grouping data into predefined ranges
- Ranking results
- Inserting calculated fields

In addition to the above, you will also learn **how to create and update a basic Dashboard** using Pivot Table data.

VLOOKUP formula

Next, we'll take a look at another powerful formula from Microsoft® Excel® called the **'VLOOKUP'**. The VLOOKUP formula allows you to search for and return a value from one Excel® list to a new Excel® spreadsheet based on a *matching lookup value*.

The field you want to find (match) is typically located on another tab or spreadsheet.

In the example below, **'A2'** is selected which has the Sales Person ID value of **'200'**. I will look to match this value on the tab labeled **'Sheet2'**. **Sales Person Name** is the value I want to look-up and be returned to the tab labeled **'Sheet1'**.

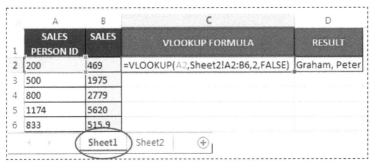

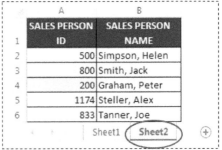

IF & NESTED IF formulas

Lastly, let's review some formulas included as part of Microsoft's®
logic functionality. The most common are **'IF'** & **'NESTED IF'**
formulas.

- **IF** formulas allow you test conditions and return one value *if
  true* and another *if false.*
- **NESTED IF** formulas allow you test conditions and return one
  value *if true* and another *if false, if* certain criteria is met.

----

*Example of a basic **IF formula**, here we're comparing the results of
two datasets:*

- *If* the results match between the two datasets, indicate with
  the word **'Pass'**
- *If* the results DO NOT match, display with the word **'Fail'**

F2	▼	:	✕	✓	*fx*	=IF(B2=D2,"Pass","Fail")

	A	B	C	D	E	F
1	RESULTS 1	COUNT	RESULTS 2	COUNT		If results match, indicate with the word "Pass"
2	Test #1	111	Test #1	111		Pass
3	Test #2	161	Test #2	158		Fail

*Example of a **NESTED IF formula**, here we're evaluating if a sales person needs additional training based on their closing sales percentage:*

The criteria for our evaluation is as follows, for sales closing percent:

- 85% or higher = **Achiever**
- 70 – 84%   = **Meeting Expectations**
- 69% or less   = **Needs Training**

=IF(E3>=0.85,"Achiever",IF(E3>=0.7,"Meeting Expectations",IF(E3>=0.69,"Needs Training","Needs Training")))

	D	E	F	G	H	I	J
	SALES PERSON	% OF CLOSED SALES	85%< Achiever 70 - 84%> Meets Expectations 69%< Needs Additional Training				
	Dower, John	60%	Needs Training				
	Wilson, John	75%	Meeting Expectations				
	Williams, Abbey	77%	Meeting Expectations				
	Taylor, Sarah	70%	Meeting Expectations				
	Graham, Peter	88%	Achiever				
	Simpson, Helen	49%	Needs Training				
	Smith, Jack	70%	Meeting Expectations				
	Steller, Alex	85%	Achiever				
	Tanner, Joe	80%	Meeting Expectations				
	Winchester, Billy	66%	Needs Training				

While the above was not a comprehensive list of all the intermediate formulas and features available in Microsoft® Excel®, I hoped it peaked your interest to the many things Excel® can do beyond basic formulas and lists!

CHAPTER 15

Microsoft® Excel® Shortcuts

The following lists some of the most common Microsoft® Excel® shortcuts:

DESCRIPTION	COMMANDS
FORMATTING	
CTRL+B	Applies or removes **bold** formatting
CTRL+I	Applies or removes *italic* formatting
CTRL+U	Applies or removes underlining formatting
FUNCTION	
CTRL+A	Selects (highlights) the entire worksheet
CTRL+C	Copies the contents of selected (highlighted) cells
CTRL+X	Cuts the selected cells
CTRL+V	Pastes the contents of selected (highlighted) cells, including cell formatting
CTRL+F	Displays the Find and Replace dialog box, with the **Find** tab selected
CTRL+H	Displays the Find and Replace dialog box, with the **Replace** tab selected
CTRL+K	Displays the Insert Hyperlink dialog box for new hyperlinks or the Edit Hyperlink dialog box for selected existing hyperlinks
CTRL+N	Creates a new blank workbook
CTRL+O	Displays the dialog box to open a file
CTRL+S	Saves the active file with its current file name, location, and file format
CTRL+P	Displays the Print dialog box
CTRL+Z	The undo function will reverse the last command or to delete the last entry you typed
ESC	Cancels an entry in the active cell or 'Formula Bar'

Shortcuts continued:

NAVIGATION	
CTRL+PageUp	Switches between worksheet tabs, from **right-to-left**
CTRL+PageDown	Switches between worksheet tabs, from **left-to-right**
CTRL+↓	Goes to the last row with content for the active column
CTRL+↑	Goes to the first row with content for the active column
CTRL+→	Goes to the last column with content for the active row
CTRL+Home	Goes to cell A1 of the active worksheet
Shift + F3	Opens the Excel formula window
EDITING	
F7	Runs Spellcheck
Shift + F7	Opens the thesaurus dialogue box

Glossary

TERM	DESCRIPTION
Access® MS Access® Microsoft® Access®	Access® is part of the Microsoft® Office® suite, the database application
Add-Ins	Add-Ins are optional tabs that provide additional and more advanced Excel® functionality.
Cell	A Cell holds one piece of information such as a number, currency value, date, text, or formula.
Excel® MS Excel® Microsoft® Excel®	Excel® is the spreadsheet program that allows users to organize, calculate, track, and perform analysis on virtually any type of data.
Formula	A formula calculates numbers or evaluates the contents of one or more cells.
Function	A function in Excel® is a predefined formula. An example of a function name is 'Count'.
OneNote® Microsoft® OneNote ®	OneNote® is part of the Microsoft® Office® suite, a program that stores text, web links, images and other information in one place
Outlook® MS Outlook ® Microsoft® Outlook ®	Part of the Microsoft® Office® suite, an email application
Pivot Tables	Pivot Tables use built-in filters and functions to quickly organize, summarize, and filter large amounts of records.
PowerPoint® MS PowerPoint ® Microsoft® PowerPoint ®	PowerPoint® is part of the Microsoft® Office® suite, a presentation / slideshow program
Publisher® MS Publisher® Microsoft® Publisher®	Publisher® is part of the Microsoft® Office® suite, a tool to create professional looking flyers, advertisements, brochures, invitations etc.

Glossary continued:

Syntax	Syntax in Excel® refers to the arrangement or order of a formula or function. All formulas & functions begin with the equal sign (=) followed by numbers or the function's name.
Word® MS Word® Microsoft® Word®	Word® is part of the Microsoft® Office® suite, a word processing application
Workbook	A Workbook file is made up of one or more worksheets. Worksheets are also referred to as tabs.

Appendix A

Add-Ins

Name and description of the more popular Excel® Add-Ins:

Add-In	DESCRIPTION
Analysis ToolPak	Used for engineering and statistical analysis. Some of the more common types of examination: • Anova • Correlation • Covariance • Descriptive Statistics • Histogram • Moving Average • Random Number Generation • Rank and Percentile • Regression • Sampling • t-Test
Developer	Developer, *is not* an add-In, instead it is a tab you can activate. Often used when creating and modifying macros. Also, includes form and ActiveX controls (buttons & list boxes).
PowerPivot	Power Pivot allows you to import millions of rows of data from multiple data sources into a single Excel® workbook, create calculated columns and measures using formulas, or build PivotTables and PivotCharts
Power Query	Power Query is part of Microsoft's® Business Intelligence self-service solution, used for analysis and to search for data from a wide variety of data sources.

A MESSAGE FROM THE AUTHOR

Thank you!

Thank you for purchasing and reading this book, I hope you found it helpful! Your feedback is valued and appreciated! Please take a few minutes and leave a review.

OTHER BOOKS AVAILABLE FROM THIS AUTHOR

- The Step-By-Step Guide To The **25 Most Common** Microsoft® Excel® Formulas & Features

- The **Step-By-Step** Guide To **Pivot Tables &** Introduction To **Dashboards**

- The Step-By-Step Guide To The **VLOOKUP** formula in Microsoft® Excel®

- The Microsoft® Excel® Step-By-Step Training Guide **Book Bundle**

www.ingramcontent.com/pod-product-compliance
Lightning Source LLC
Chambersburg PA
CBHW070849070326
40690CB00009B/1767